THE HEROIC ADVENTURES OF HOPE THE HIPPO

All profits donated to Lily's Hope Foundation

**Jennifer M. Driscoll
Lilian Hope Driscoll
and Aidan Patrick Driscoll**

Illustrations by Art Knute

©2020 by Lily's Hope Foundation

All rights reserved. No part of this publication may be reproduced or transmitted in any form or by any means, electronic or mechanical, including photocopying, recording, or any other information storage and retrieval system, without the written permission of the publisher.

Printed in the United States of America

Published in Hellertown, PA

Cover and interior design and illustrations by Art Knute

ISBN 978-1-950459-20-9

2 4 6 8 10 9 7 5 3 1 paperback

MomosaPublishing.com

When siblings Lily and Aidan were born early, they spent time in the hospital. After their experience, their family started a non-profit organization called Lily's Hope Foundation, which helps families with premature babies in the NICU.

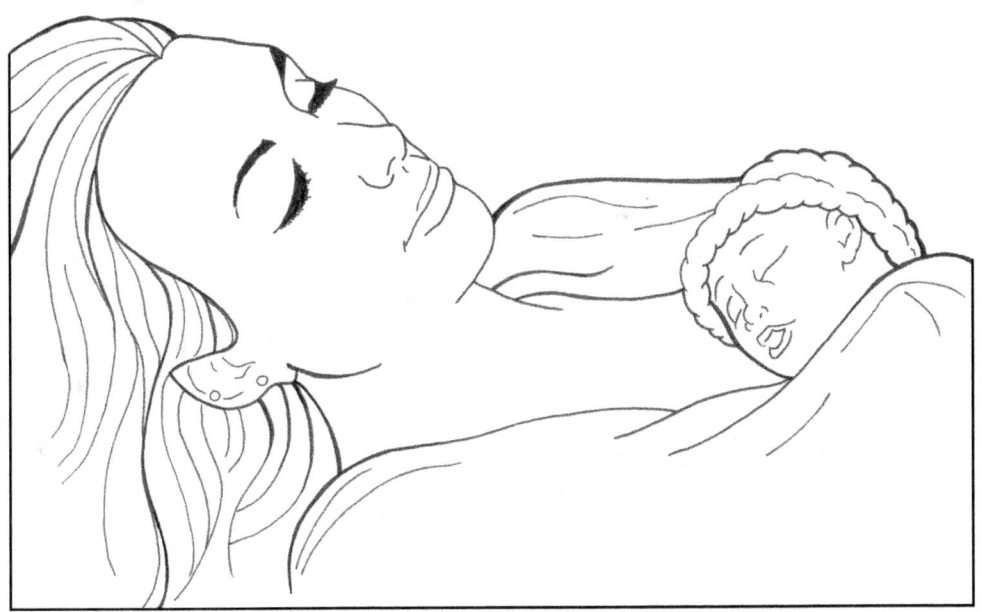

Lily and Aidan's friend, Hope the Hippo, was born at Lily's Hope Foundation in Allentown, Pennsylvania, a place where people offer aid and hope to families of premature babies. Hope wanted to help these families, too.

Hope the Hippo was excited to go to the Lily's Hope Foundation Packing Party. Dozens of volunteers worked together to create care packages for families of premature babies. Hope's journey began by being tucked inside a box for a new baby, along with diapers, clothing, and other helpful items.

Complete the Picture

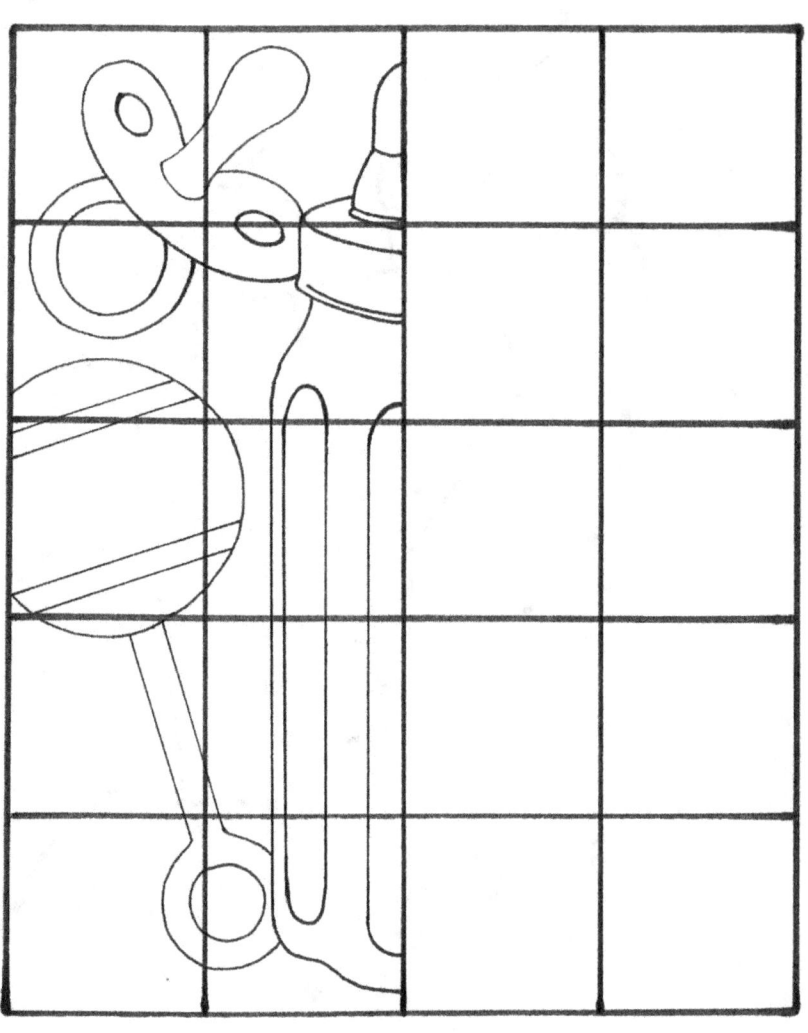

Hope was tired from the long trip and excited to get home and meet the new family. Hope looked forward to sharing the items in the care package with the baby.

After a good night's sleep Hope went with the new family to the hospital to meet the baby. Hope was excited to begin their journey together.

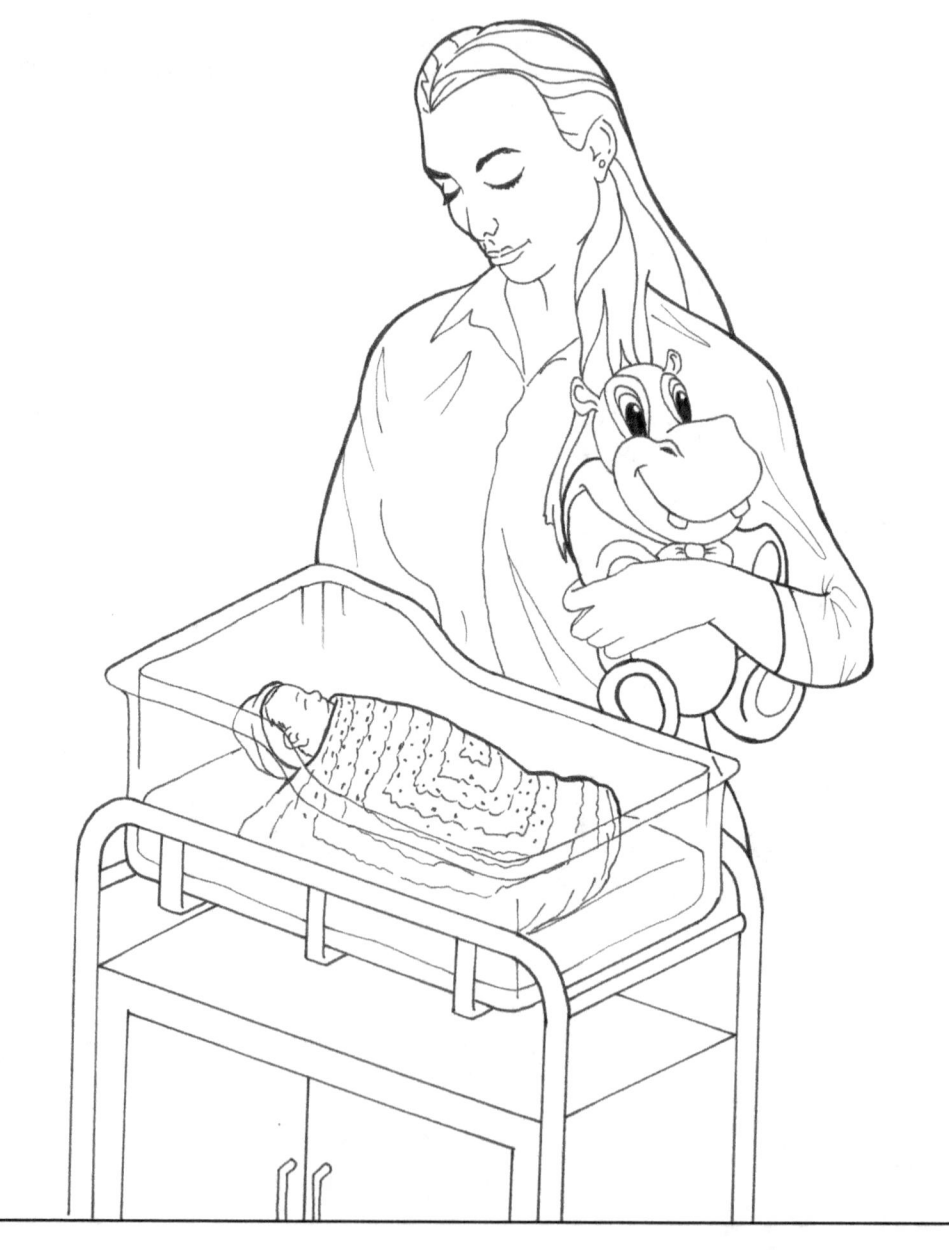

Color by Number

1 = Black   2 = Grey   3 = Light Grey
4 = Pink   5 = Red   6 = Yellow

Hope was soon tucked into bed beside the baby.
The bed was quite comfy, and Hope loved
being close to the tiny baby.

Maze

Help Hope get to the baby.

Hope loved watching the baby grow bigger and stronger every day! Hope could tell that the NICU nurses and doctors cared very much about the baby and wanted to see the baby grow, too.

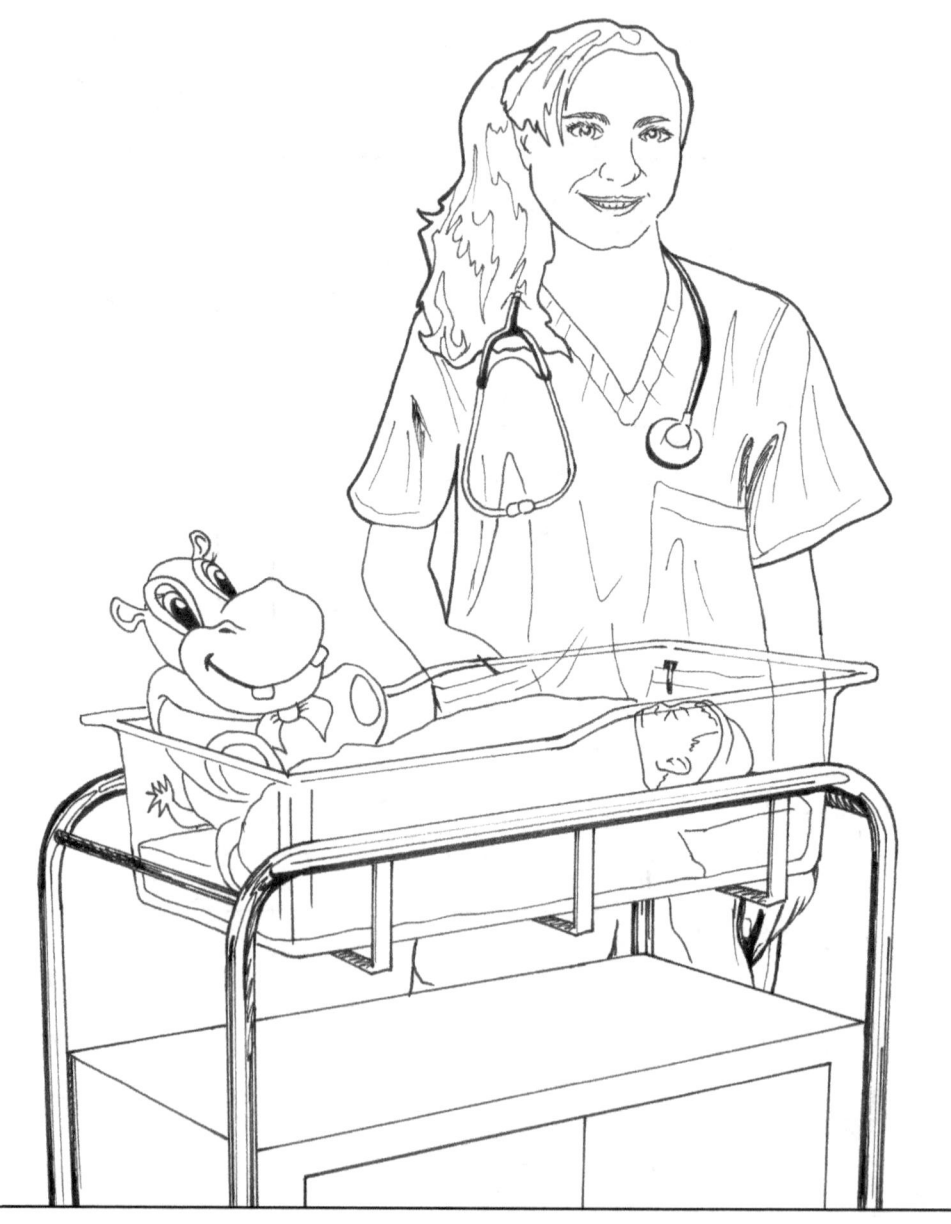

Word Search

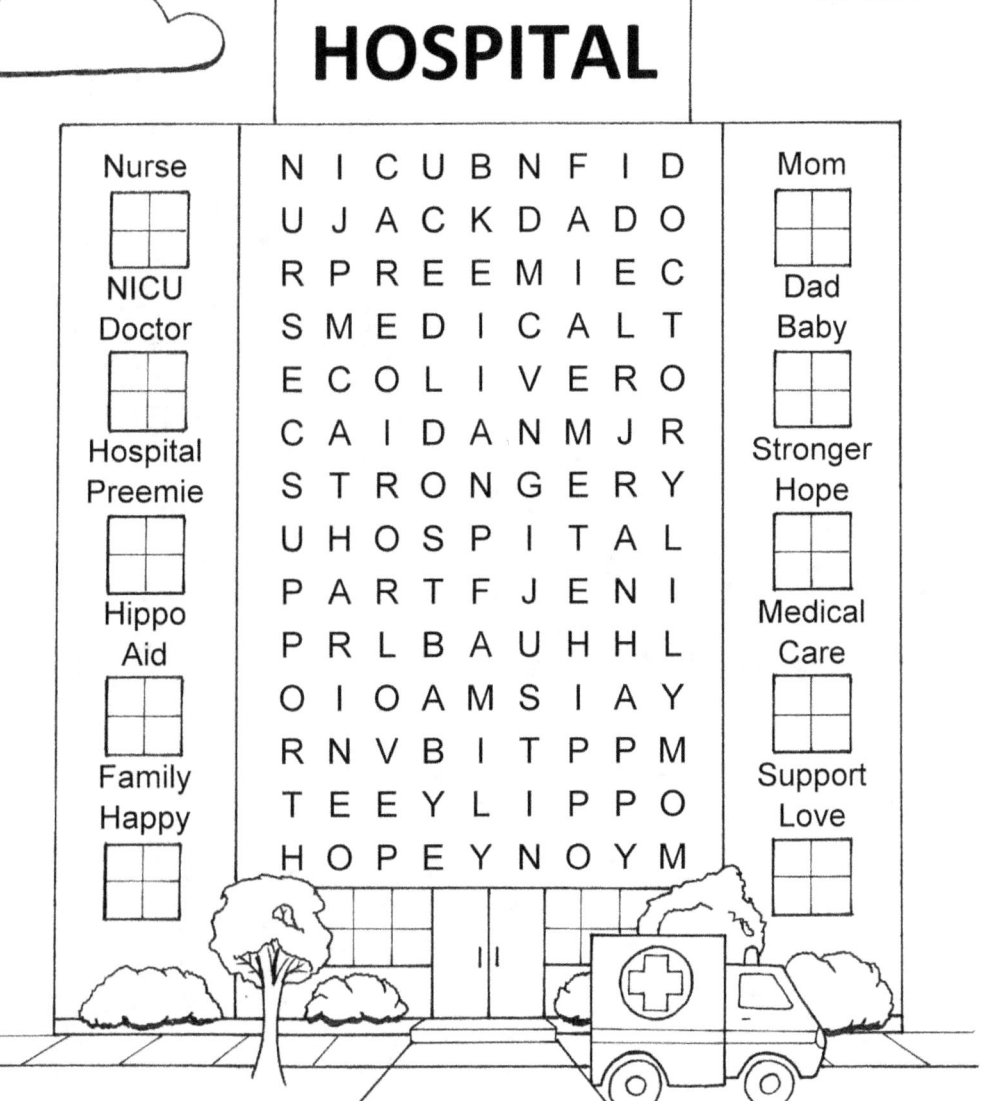

Answers on the last page.

After a few weeks in the NICU, the baby had grown big and strong enough to go home. Hope went along and settled into a healthy routine with the family.

As Hope watched, the baby began achieving milestones: smiling, rolling over, and sitting up. Sometimes it takes longer for premature babies to reach milestones, but Hope supported the baby along the way.

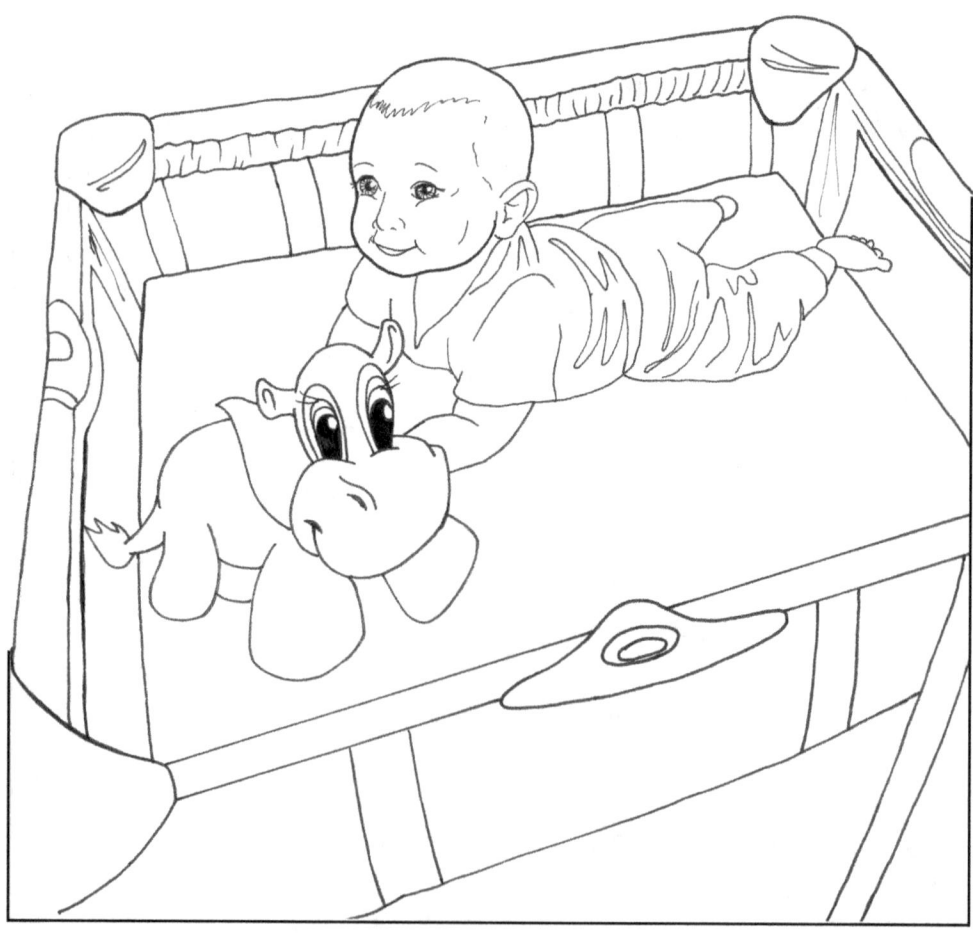

Connect the Dots

Hope especially loved going on outings with the family. They went on hikes, to the zoo, and even to ball games.

Tic-Tac-Toe

Dots: Take turns connecting dots. If you make a square, put your initial inside, and go again. The player with the most squares wins!

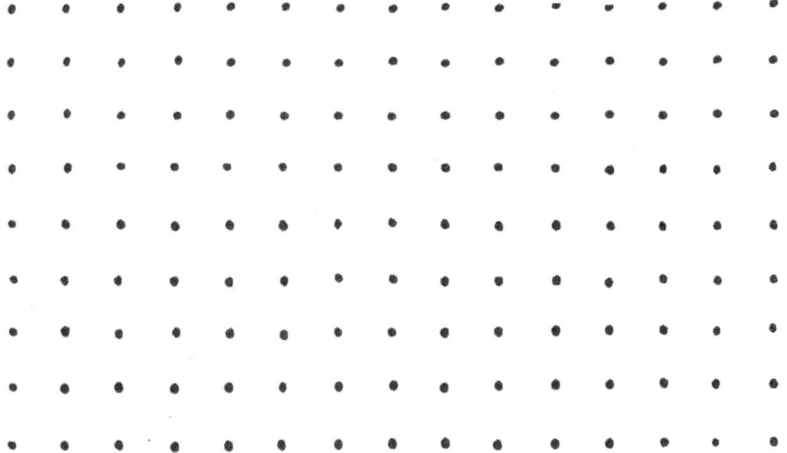

A special time for Hope was when the family flew back across the country to a Lily's Hope event!

The family attended Lily's Loop, held at the Valley Preferred Cycling Center in Breinigsville, Pennsylvania.

Hope and the family enjoyed celebrating the baby's first holidays, Halloween, Thanksgiving, and Christmas.

Which one does not belong?

1.
2.
3.
4.
5.

Hooray! Hope and the baby celebrated their first birthday and journey together with cake and ice cream. Happy birthday, baby! Happy Birthday, Hope the Hippo!

Word Scramble

1. eakc   _ _ _ _

2. npsetres   _ _ _ _ _ _ _ _

3. baydihtr   _ _ _ _ _ _ _ _

4. cie eracm   _ _ _ _ _ _ _ _

5. dnacle   _ _ _ _ _ _

6. cetearelb   _ _ _ _ _ _ _ _ _

7. bolosaln   _ _ _ _ _ _ _ _

8. rypat   _ _ _ _ _

9. neo   _ _ _

10. phpya   _ _ _ _ _

Answers on the last page.

Draw Your Own Story Here

Tips for Parents

Here are some tips from parents of preemies on how to ease your transition home from the hospital.

Be patient. As much as you're looking forward to that glorious day when you get to take your baby home, know that babies in the NICU typically aren't sent home until they're off medications and oxygen. Fortunately, you should be given plenty of notice before the big day so you can prepare and plan.

Stock up on preemie diapers. In addition to all the supplies needed for any newborn baby, you'll want to stock up on preemie-sized diapers and clothing.

Room-in if possible. Some hospitals allow parents to stay in a special room with their baby at the hospital the night before going home. This simulates the home environment, especially since your baby will likely be sleeping in the same room with you for the first four to six months. Just make sure your baby sleeps in a crib or bassinet, not in your bed with you.

Ask about a car bed. Often premature babies are sent home in a special car bed, rather than in a car seat. The nurses in the NICU will administer a car seat test for safety. If your baby needs a car bed, a social worker will coordinate this for you through your insurance company.

Get mentally prepared. Envision yourselves at home, finally having your baby all to yourself without nurses or wires or beeping machines.

Get pets ready. Before you bring your baby home, introduce your little one's scent by bringing a blanket home from the NICU for your dog or cat to smell.

Be ready for unexpected challenges. If you're the parents of multiples, be prepared for the possibility that one of your babies might come home before the others. Try to plan ahead for how you will juggle caring for your baby at home and also commuting to the hospital and spending time there.

Ask questions. Make sure all discharge info is clearly documented so you know all about any referrals, follow-up appointments, and prescriptions.

About Lily's Hope Foundation

Lily's Hope Foundation is a 501(c)(3) nonprofit organization that answers the emergency needs of families with premature babies. Lily's Hope accomplishes this by providing resources, aid, and hope to families with premature babies through our Preemie Pantry and our Packages of Hope program.

Lily's Hope Foundation aids and empowers NICU families with urgent and unexpected needs by providing essential items they may lack because they were unable to prepare for their child's early arrival. Our Lily's Hope Foundation Families who are in the middle of this medical crisis are referred to us by hospital case workers, hospital staff, and word of mouth. We work with each family to answer their specific needs through our Packages of Hope, which include items that can often be expensive and difficult to find. Examples of the care package contents are micro-preemie/preemie clothing, preemie diapers, car seats or car seat beds, bassinets, gift cards for use toward transportation to the NICU, and more. Lily's Hope® and Lily's Loop® are registered trademarks with the United States Patent and Trademark Office. Lily's Hope Foundation has published two other books, Lily's Hope: A Preemie's Journey of Hope, which is a book for children, and Preemie Parents' Tips to Get You Thru the NICU, a book filled with tips and advice for parents. For more information, please visit our website LilysHopeFoundation.org.

Word search answer key

```
N I C U B N F I D
U J A C K D A D O
R P R E E M I E C
S M E D I C A L T
E C O L I V E R O
C A I D A N M J R
S T R O N G E R Y
U H O S P I T A L
P A R T F J E N I
P R L B A U H H L
O I O A M S I A Y
R N V B I T P P M
T E E Y L I P P O
H O P E Y N O Y M
```

Word scramble answers

1. Cake
2. Presents
3. Birthday
4. Ice cream
5. Candle
6. Celebrate
7. Balloons
8. Party
9. One
10. Happy

www.ingramcontent.com/pod-product-compliance
Lightning Source LLC
Chambersburg PA
CBHW052130110526
44592CB00013B/1818